Independent London
Guide

D1631036

EAST
LONDON
Edition

Perhaps the best known area of East London, Shoreditch offers a diverse mix of independent stores, a busy nightlife, chic galleries and a multitude of popular eateries, bars, clubs and cafés. Famous for its colourful street art, creative community, arty vibe and selection of shopping, Red Church Street is one of the most popular streets in the area offering a perfect cross-section of everything this neighbourhood is known (and loved) for.

INDEPENDENT

Shoreditch

8   **PITFIELD LONDON** 31-35 Pitfield Street, Shoreditch N1 6HB
020 7490 6852   www.pitfieldlondon.com

Glamorous ever evolving concept store, gallery and café. Perfect for
the ultimate home store rummage followed with coffee and a pastry.

9 **CYCLELAB & JUICE BAR** 18a Pitfield Street, Shoreditch N1 6EY
020 3222 0016 www.cyclelab.co.uk

Juice bar, café, bike shop (Ritte and Cinelli) and drop in repair service,
have a crêpe while you wait. You can even hire their cycle powered juicer.

MADE IN RATIO 16 Holywell Row, Shoreditch EC2A 4XA
020 7247 8009 www.madeinratio.com

Fusing art and design, Made in Ratio manufactures bold and contemporary furniture and lighting, with a focus on form, function, minimalism and geometric shapes.

11 PASSIONE VINO 85 Leonard Street, Shoreditch EC2A 4QS
020 3487 0600 www.passionevino.co.uk

This passionate duo are specialising in small wine producers, providing an impressive range of the very best of authentic and artisan wines from Italy.

12   **BOTTEGA PRELIBATO** 45 Rivington Street, Shoreditch EC2A 3QB
020 7739 4995 www.bottegaprelibato.com

Intimate Italian restaurant, deli and gallery (work by local Hackney artists) serving delicacies such as burrata, salty-sweet parma ham and handmade pappardelle.

13 **TUK** 47 Rivington Street, Shoreditch EC2A 3QB
020 3417 6335 www.tukstore.org

Outlet for a community interest company shop, focused on improving communities, selling unique products by artists with all profits funding community objectives.

BLOOD BROTHER 10 Charlotte Road, Shoreditch EC2A 3DH
020 7729 5005 www.blood-brother.co.uk

Bold, cool and black – Blood brother is a menswear brand collaboration of photographers, film makers and music artists, under the maxim 'Never Alone'.

15 **GOODHOOD** 151 Curtain Road, Shoreditch EC2A 3QE
020 7729 3600 www.goodhoodstore.com

A multi-level creative concept store championing independent fashion, interiors and beauty labels, Goodhood is an East London shopping emporium not to be missed.

YCN 72 Rivington Street, Shoreditch EC2A 3AY
020 7033 2140 www.ycn.org

Showcasing the work of emerging designers and illustrators, creative agency
YCN sells a mix of limited-edition prints, posters, cards and wrapping paper.

17 **MJM** 1st Floor, 17a Kingsland Road, Shoreditch E2 8AA
020 7739 3699 www.makinjanma.com

Hong Kong-born RCA graduate Makin Jan Ma's concept store sells quirky unisex fashion with a focus on over-sized silhouettes, creative prints and bold colours.

HOUSE OF LIZA 9 Pearson Street, Hoxton E2 8JD
020 3487 0782   www.houseofliza.co.uk

Stocking a high-end vintage fashion collection of focusing on the 1970s–90s,
this gallery-like space is a haven for stylists, fashionistas and vintage lovers.

19 **BETTER HEALTH BAKERY** 13 Stean Street, Haggerston E8 4ED
020 7254 9103 www.centreforbetterhealth.org.uk

There's nothing better for the soul than baking bread, as the volunteers of this bakery, which is a charity promoting mental well being would be happy to confirm.

2 & 4 2-4 Southgate Road, Hoxton N1 3JJ
020 7254 5202 www.2mdesign.co.uk

Known for its signature use of bold primary colours and cutting edge materials, this contemporary design and vintage store is home to British interiors label 2M.

21 **MILK CONCEPT BOUTIQUE** 118 1/2 Shoreditch High Street, Shoreditch E1 6JN
020 7729 9880 www.milkconceptboutique.co.uk

Housed in an 18th century historic building, this design concept boutique stocks independent fashion labels as well as a Fornasetti homeware.

22 **SNEAKERS N STUFF** 107-108 Shoreditch High Street, Shoreditch E1 6JN
020 3754 6443 www.sneakersnstuff.com

Stocking a mix of streetwear and on-trend trainers, Sneakersnstuff offers labels
including Nike and Converse as well as exclusive limited-edition collaborations.

23 **ACE HOTEL** 100 Shoreditch High Street, Shoreditch E1 6JQ
020 7613 9800 www.acehotel.com

With it's mix of art, designer objects, vinyl, good coffee and the Hoi Polloi restaurant, Ace has become one of the most popular hangout spots in Shoreditch.

24 **FORGE & CO** 154–158 Shoreditch High Street, Shoreditch E1 6HU
020 7729 0007 www.forgeandco.co.uk

Housed in a 1950s modernist office block, Forge & Co is a creative events
and gallery space, with a restaurant which serves a modern British menu.

25 **MAIDEN** 188 Shoreditch High Street, Shoreditch E1 6HU
020 7998 0185 www.maidenshop.com

Fun and quirky design objects you never knew you wanted, including gifts, stationery, home accessories, books and jewellery at this contemporary boutique.

GLASSWORKS

GLASSWORKS 190 Shoreditch High Street, Shoreditch E2 7DP
08454 100 110 www.glassworks-studios.com

Typifying the very essence of East London cool, Glassworks is a cutting-edge womenswear brand with a bold statement pieces and avant-garde accessories.

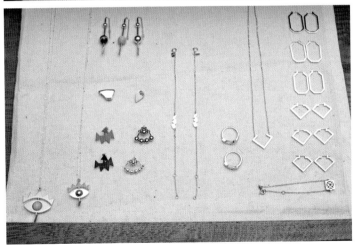

27 **CELESTINE ELEVEN** 4 Holywell Lane, Shoreditch E2 7DJ
020 7729 2987 www.celestineeleven.com

With an emphasis on holistic health and mindful living, this beautiful concept store houses a well-considered selection of unusual high-end designers for women.

LOUNGE BOHEMIA 1e Great Eastern Street, Shoreditch EC2A 3EJ
07720 707 000 www.loungebohemia.com

A hidden gem, the stylish cocktail bar offers an avant-garde selection of cocktails and Czech-inspired canapés complete with charming, retro interiors. Booking only.

29 **APC** 15 Redchurch Street, Shoreditch E2 7DJ
020 7729 7727 www.apc.com

French fashion favourite, A.P.C. provides chic pared-down basics for both women and men with minimalist staples such as Breton-striped sweaters and stylish denim.

30 **AIMÉ** 17 Redchurch Street E2 7DP
020 7739 2158 www.aimelondon.com

Showing the best of French design, the womenswear boutique stocks a well-curated selection of Parisian fashion brands such as cult labels Isabel Marant and Repetto.

31 **CHAAT** 36 Redchurch Street, Shoreditch E2 7DJ
020 7739 9595 www.chaatlondon.co.uk

Fusing art with food, this cozy Bangladeshi gallery/café/restaurant serves authentic dishes such as fish moilee, chili beef and classic lamb keema.

32 **MAISON TROIS GARCONS** 45 Redchurch Street, Shoreditch E2 7DJ
020 3370 7761 www.lestroisgarcons.com

A fabulous mix of antiques, vintage fashion accessories and decorative objects, make this one-of-a-kind café the perfect destination for vintage and design lovers.

33 **BURRO E SALVIA** 52 Redchurch Street, Shoreditch E2 7DP
020 7739 4429 www.burroesalvia.co.uk

Passionate about Fresh pasta, this small contemporary Italian deli makes authentic pasta with delights such as butter and sage stuffed ravioli and classic penne.

IN HOUSE 67 Redchurch Street, Shoreditch E2 7DP
020 7729 5117 www.inhousestudios.co.uk

Ever-evolving concept store and experimental gallery space, changing the themes of its retail space monthly, with creative subjects varying from food, art and design.

35 **SEVENTYFIVE BY MK2UK** 75 Redchurch Street, Shoreditch E2 7DJ
info@mk2uk.com www.mk2uk.com

This unique contemporary fashion concept store carries minimalist unisex pieces and edgy accessories featuring cutting edge silhouettes and unusual design details.

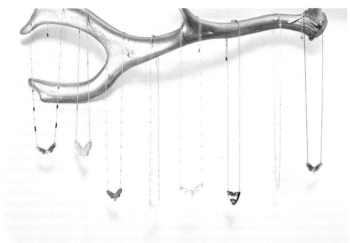

36 **THOR & WISTLE** 5a Club Row, Shoreditch E1 5ES
020 7566 8777 www.thorandwistle.com

Inspired by mythology and symbolism, this whimsical independent jewellery gallery and workshop stocks an array of handmade gems as well as bespoke pieces.

LES TROIS GARCONS 1 Club Row, Shoreditch E1 6JX
020 7613 1924 www.lestroisgarcons.com

Over-sized crystal chandeliers and a stuffed giraffe – when it comes to quirky, lush interiors and taxidermy, more is definitely more at this French gourmet restaurant.

ELEMENTARY 77 Redchurch Street, Shoreditch E2 7DP
020 3487 0980 www.elementarystore.co.uk

This bright and airy gallery-like design boutique carries a range of minimalist home and tableware including elegant wine decanters and contemporary ceramics.

MONOLOGUE 93 Redchurch Street, Shoreditch E2 7DJ
020 7729 0400 www.monologuelondon.com

With design products by established interiors brands as well as new and upcoming, this concept store stocks a contemporary edit of stylish homeware and furniture.

40 **VINTAGE GUITAR BOUTIQUE** 49 Bethnal Green Road, Shoreditch E1 6LA
020 7729 9186   www.vintageguitarboutique.com

Specialist boutique with an outstanding array of vintage, rare guitars and amps.
The American vintage guitar collection is one of the best in London.

LABOUR AND WAIT 85 Redchurch Street, Shoreditch E2 7DJ
020 7729 6253 www.labourandwait.co.uk

Selling a handpicked selection of functional and stylish home products and clothing, timeless design and craftsmanship lie at the very core of this traditional store.

LARACHE 30–32 Calvert Avenue, Shoreditch E2 7JP
020 7729 7349 www.hassanhajjaj.com

Founder and owner of Larache, Hassan Hajjaj, handpicks and imports a variety of
treasures from Morocco including traditional lamps, cushions, bags and jewellery.

43 **SOBOYE** 13 Calvert Avenue, Shoreditch E2 7JP
020 7729 3521 www.soboye.com

Africa cool! Funky, playful, stylish African prints and colours, Soboye stocks own brand and guest labels for women and men as well as gifts and textiles for the home.

LUNA & CURIOUS 24–26 Calvert Avenue, Shoreditch E2 7DJ
020 7033 4411 www.lunaandcurious.com.com

A lifestyle concept store, L & C houses a whimsical mix of tableware, fashion, books and magazines. It also sells an adorable handpicked selection of kidswear.

O'DELL'S 24 Calvert Avenue, Shoreditch E2 7DJ
07730 129 416 www.odellsstore.com

Home to a stylish mix of menswear, accessories and interiors. Favourites include eyewear by Danish brand Han Kjøbenhavn and skincare products by Honest.

46 **CHARLENE MULLEN** 7 Calvert Avenue, Shoreditch E2 7JP
020 7739 6987 www.charlenemullen.com

Mixing quirky humor with geometric shapes and classic folk motifs, Charlene Mullen creates unique embroidered textiles fueled by a passion for illustration and print.

47 **SEH KELLY** 1 Cleve Workshops, Boundary Street, Shoreditch E2 7JD
020 3397 0449 www.sehkelly.com

Passionate about heritage design and traditional craftsmanship, this British menswear label make a range of classic garments with a modern twist.

With a diverse mix of local Londoners, tourists, students and creative types – Brick Lane is an East London focal point, perhaps best known for its many curry houses and busy Sunday markets. Scratch the surface, however, and discover an authentic part of the East End, complete with classic Victorian and Georgian architecture, independent galleries and a diverse, ever-evolving food scene.

INDEPENDENT

Brick Lane

52 **CHEZ ELLES** 45 Brick Lane E1 6PU
020 7247 9699 www.chezellesbistroquet.co.uk

With a menu consisting of traditional French cooking (steak tartare, onion soup, foie grass, mussels), an adorable bistro evoking a little bit of Paris on the Brick Lane.

53 **BLITZ** 55–59 Hanbury Street, Brick Lane E1 5JP
020 7377 0730 www.blitzlondon.com

Vintage grand emporium over several floors in a former furniture factory
with a wow factor putting many vintage shops in the shade.

LIK + NEON 106 Sclater Street, Brick Lane E1 6HR
020 7729 4650 www.likneon.com

The original shop with cats! Always changing collection of mostly local
artists work, all unique from jewellery and t-shirts to books, prints and cards.

55 HARNETT & POPE 125 Brick Lane E1 6SB
www.harnettandhope.com

Local London fashion at its best, Harnett & Pope's original womenswear consists of unusual silhouettes, bold colours, unique patterns and eye-catching prints.

THE LAMPLIGHTER.

With her imaginative and quirky jewellery designs, Amy Anderson has grown a loyal following since opening this enchanting and elegant independent boutique in 2004.

57 **JIMBOBART** 24 Cheshire Street, Brick Lane E2 6EH
07862 276 096 www.jimbobart.com

Channeling the very best of English eccentricity, illustrator James Ward's contemporary ceramics and prints feature a range of humorous animal drawings.

LOST LAUNDRY 28 Cheshire Street, Brick Lane E2 6EH
020 7729 4882 www.lostlaundry.co.uk

With a selection of high-end fashion, Lost Laundry sells past season collections from designers such as Jonathan Saunders, Proenza Schouler and Alexander McQueen.

59 **COCK & BULL** 30 Cheshire Street, Brick Lane E2 6EH
020 7729 5068 www.cockandbullmenswear.co.uk

Sustainable, ethical production is at the core of C & B's ethos, supplying dapper gents with everything from tweed flat caps, hemp denim to stylish accessories.

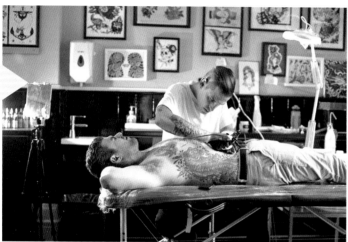

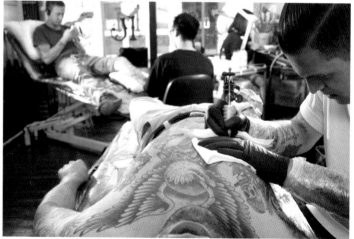

CLOAK & DAGGER 34 Cheshire Street, Brick Lane E2 6EH
0207 175 0133 www.cloakanddaggerlondon.co.uk

One stop shop for the viking, celt, saxon or ork in you. Get tooled amd costumed up to museum standards or for LARP 'live action role play' if you didn't already know.

61 PAXTON CHOCOLATE 38 Cheshire Street, Brick Lane E2 6EH
020 8127 8807 www.paxtonchocolate.com

Beautiful handmade jewel-like chocolates almost too pretty to eat. Foodies will
be tempted to attend one of its popular chocolate making workshops.

SPECSTACULAR 40 Cheshire Street, Brick Lane E2 6EH
020 3645 1237 www.specstacular.london

With a fabulous mix of vintage and contemporary eyewear, this specialist boutique provides a stylish mix of cool specs as well as eye examinations and repairs.

LUREM 138 Bethnal Green Road, Brick Lane E2 6DG
020 8127 8338 www.lurem-uk.com

Inspired by contemporary street fashion, Lurem is a Japan-based label with a sleek
minimalist aesthetic. Signature pieces of stylish outerwear, dresses and jumpers.

64   **THE LONDON FABRIC SHOP** 141 Bethnal Green Road, Brick Lane E2 7DG
0207 739 5699 www.londonfabricshop.com

The London fabric shop offers the very best of European-made textiles including
a high-end selection of beautiful linens, cottons, jacquards and jerseys.

65 **STORY PIZZA** 123 Bethnal Green Road (entrance Brick Lane) E2 7DG
07918 197 352 www.storydeli.com

Fusing industrial-style chic with bohemian rustic influences, this stylish restaurant serves authentic organic Italian pizza with Lee's own contemporary twist.

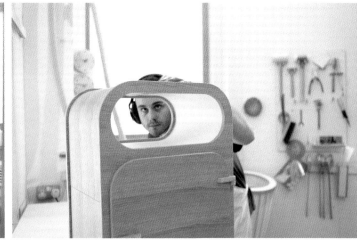

Innovative furniture maker with a wide range of products from tables to shelving and light shades. Many of their designs can be seen in the areas bars, shops and cafés.

67 TATTY DEVINE 236 Brick Lane E2 7EB
020 7739 9191 www.tattydevine.com

With signature pieces such as laser-cut Perspex statement necklaces, this trend setting costume jewellery studio offers fashion-forward and colourful accessories.

One of the fastest evolving areas in East London, Spitalfields has seen major gentrification over recent years with its close proximity to the city and financial district perhaps being one of the main contributing factors. Still full of charm, Old Spitalfields market attracts a diverse crowd of stalls, including local designers, artists and vintage dealers. The antique market on Thursdays offers a glimpse into old London and an opportunity for treasure hunters to pick up a bargain.

INDEPENDENT
SPITALFIELDS

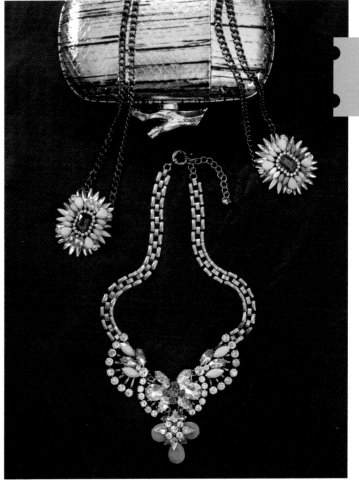

71 **PRECIOUS** 16 Artillery Passage, Spitalfields E1 7LJ
020 7377 6668 www.precious-london.com

This independent womenswear boutique offering contemporary fashion classics including statement pieces by Diane Von Furstenberg, Malene Birger and Carven.

72 ANGELA FLANDERS 4 Artillery Passage, Spitalfields E1 7LJ
020 7247 7040 www.angelaflanders-perfumer.com

Local Londoner Angela Flanders' second boutique, a chic perfumery with more than 35 unique perfumes, scented candles and elegant bath & body products.

73 **JOSHUA KANE** 53 Brushfield Street, Spitalfields E1 6AA
020 7247 6463 www.joshuakanebespoke.com

'Neo-dandy tailor', Joshua Kane combines classic tailoring with contemporary design details in British made collection of bespoke atire for today's 'Beau Brummell'.

Gallery, café and antique shop, located in an 18th century Hugenot building in the heart of Spitalfields blends in and reflects perfectly the rich history of the district.

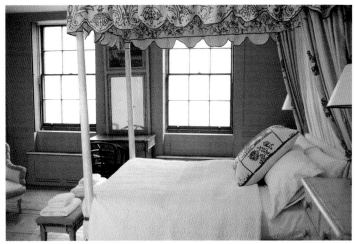

75 **STAY IN SPITALFIELDS** 5 Fournier Street, Spitalfields E1 6QE
020 7247 4745 www.stayinspitalfields.com

For a truly unique London experience, stay in this lovingly restored townhouse built in 1720. The two bed house offers a tranquil setting complete with antique interiors.

JOSEPH CHEANEY & SONS 18 Lamb Street, Spitalfields E1 6EA
020 7392 2183   www.cheaney.co.uk

Dating back to 1886, this British footwear specialist handcrafts classic shoes including traditional leather oxfords and brogues for both men and women.

77 **GRESHAM BLAKE** 143 Commercial Street, Spitalfields E1 6BJ
020 7375 0365 www.greshamblake.com

Launched in Brighton in 2000, British menswear label producing tailored fashion with a quirky twist. Signature pieces include wool outerwear and bespoke tailoring.

A beautiful testament to historic London architecture, Columbia Road offers a quaint mix of independent boutiques, galleries and small cafés, pubs and restaurants. The Sunday flower market is not to be missed, a true East End establishment – the markets stalls are heaving with activity from early morning, selling a wonderful mix of plants, cut flowers and greenery.

Columbia Road

82 **THE BIRDCAGE** 80 Columbia Road, Hackney E2 7QB
020 7739 0250

Weekend local Frank Sinatras, Lionel Ritchies, George Michaels and Dolly Partons perform at this legendary karaoke night.

83 HACKNEY 186 186 Hackney Road E2 7QL
07914 670 285

Multi-purpose venue and bar in a former shoe shop with a diverse mix of live music, cocktails, spiritual/holistic health sessions as well as a photographic/film studio.

Founded by interior designer Richard Ward, this showroom/studio offers bespoke contemporary sofas and seating in a range of colourful fabrics and unusual designs.

BRAWN 49 Columbia Road E2 7RG
020 7729 5692 www.brawn.co

Sharing plates with a focus on seasonal and locally sourced ingredients as well as a
selection of natural and organic wines. (photo) Guinea fowl with summer vegetables.

ELSIE'S DROGUERIE 110 Columbia Road E2 7RG
hello@elsiesdroguerie.co.uk www.elsiesdroguerie.co.uk

Specialist shop stocking unusual household products and useful gifts for the home,
Elsie's Droguerie sells everything from pocketknives to scented candles and soaps.

87 **RYANTOWN** 126 Columbia Road E2 7RG
020 7613 1510 www.robryanstudio.com

Outlet for popular London-based artist Rob Ryan, stocks a range of eye-catching
designs including Ryan's signature paper cutouts, screen prints, tiles and books.

CHOOSING KEEPING 128 Columbia Road E2 7RG
020 7613 3842 www.properold.com

This independent boutique offers the very best in stylish, specialist stationery including beautiful handmade papers products, writing utensils and paperweights.

89 **MILAGROS** 61 Columbia Road E2 7RG
020 7613 0876 www.milagros.co.uk

A colourful Mexican boutique, Milagros sells an intriguing mix of traditional Mexican tiles, handcrafted baskets, unique glassware and unusual pieces of folk art.

90 **MASON & PAINTER** 67 Columbia Road E2 7RG
hello@masonandpainter.co.uk www.masonandpainter.co.uk

Lovely selection of vintage interiors, tableware, fabrics and gifts, Mason & Painter stocks unique items for the home including French glassware and garden furniture.

91 **A PORTUGUESE LOVE AFFAIR** 142 Columbia Road E2 7RG
020 7613 1482 www.aportugueseloveaffair.co.uk

Gorgeous lifestyle boutique celebrating all things Portuguese, you will find an
enticing variety of ceramics, gourmet food and traditional beauty products.

92 **STARTSPACE** 150 Columbia Road E2 7RG
020 7729 0522 www.masonandpainter.com

Part art gallery, part interiors boutique, part café – this creative space exhibits
and sells the work of contemporary international and UK-based artists.

93 JUMP LIKE ALICE 162 Columbia Road E2 7RG
020 8983 7873 www.jumplikealice.com

A shop like no other, JLA stocks a wonderful, ever-evolving collection of jewellery and accessories – from 50s swimming caps to wool berets and statement earrings.

Fusing bold block colours with a simple Scandinavia-inspired aesthetic, this stylish gallery-like boutique sells design objects and chic items for the home.

95 BARN THE SPOON 260 Hackney Road E2 7SJ
07950 751 811 www.barnthespoon.com

Founded in 2012, Barn sells a variety of handcrafted wooden spoons from his workshop. Attend one of his carving classes to make you're own ultimate spoon.

96 **MR BUCKLEY'S** 277 Hackney Road E2 8NA
020 3665 0033 www.mrbuckleys.com

A stylish atmospheric restaurant and cocktail bar, Mr Buckley's seasonal menu fuses traditional British cuisine with American and European influences.

97 **WALL AND JONES** 340 Hackney Road E2 7AX
020 3302 5654 www.wallandjones.com

Fusing contemporary design with vintage fabrics and silhouettes, this boutique creates bespoke and ready-to-wear fashion items with a truly unique aesthetic.

This may very well be the trendiest of all London markets with a great opportunity to spot some of the very best street fashion in the capital. The Saturday market has become extremely popular with both local hipsters and tourists, offering a splendid selection of vintage fashion, gourmet food and coffee as well as stationery, accessories and art books.

INDEPENDENT
Broadway
Market

Keeping it real in East London with t-shirt slogans like 'Keep Hackney Shit' and
'Fuck Speed Humps and Potholes' Black Skulls won't let modern life grind 'em down.

103 **MOMOSAN SHOP** 79a Wilton Way, Hackney E8 1BG
www.momosanshop.com

Beautiful utilitarian and decorative objects for the home. Sourced from Japan, Europe and the US.

Cute showcase in a former sweet shop of the kind of classic home products many may remember that were better made before the advent of extreme globalisation.

105 BOLT Arch 3, Fieldworks, 274 Richmond Road, Hackney E8 3QW
07963 747 389 www.boltlondon.com

Hidden beneath the railway arches at London Fields, Bolt is a custom motorcycle shop stocking unique fashion forward bike gear and original biker accessories.

OUTSIDER MOTORCYCLE CLUB 65 Mare Street, Hackney E8 4RG
07942 862 404 www.outsidermotorcycleclub.blogspot.co.uk

A one stop outpost for rockers, bikers, front men and rock chicks, from guitars, marshall amps, leather jackets to fedora hats and boots for strutting your stuff.

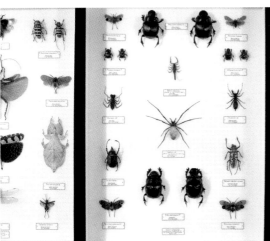

107 THE LAST TUESDAY SOCIETY 11 Mare Street, Hackney E8 4RP
020 7998 3617 www.thelasttuesdaysociety.org

A bar-café like no other, The Last Tuesday Society is a true original, home to the Museum of Curiosities, a literary salon – it even has its own taxidermy academy.

BERT & MAY 67 Vyner Street, Hackney E2 9DQ
020 3673 4264 www.bertandmay.com

A favourite with interiors stylists and designers in the know, this stunning collection of reclaimed tiles is housed in a hidden away old Victorian warehouse.

109 DOG & WARDROBE Unit 3b, Regent Studios, 8 Andrews Road E8 4QN
07966 163 064 www.thedogandwardrobe.com

Purveyor of British design heritage with a good eye for industrial reclaim and exciting mix of vintage ready for re-purposing. Always worth popping in for a browse.

110 FABRICATIONS 7 Broadway Market, Hackney E8 4PH
020 7275 8043 www.fabrications1.co.uk

Passionate about up and recycling as well as eco and sustainable design, this independent textile gallery, shop and studio is dedicated to contemporary fabrics.

Stylish, contemporary and pared down fashion for women and men, this boutique houses a selection of some of the very best UK and Scandinavian designers.

ISLE OF OLIVE 6c Ada Street, Hackney E8 4QU
020 7241 6493 www.isleofolive.co.uk

A piece of Greece in East London, Isle of Olive stocks over 200 artisan Greek
food products including traditional cheese, olives, figs and gourmet cooking oils.

113 **EAST LONDON DESIGN STORE** 6a Ada Street, Hackney E8 4QU
020 7254 3760 www.eastlondondesignstore.com

Specialising in British design, brilliant interiors and gift store offering contemporary
and often local artists prints, cards, design objects, lighting and furniture.

Dedicated to art and design, Artwords stocks an impressive selection of modern art, photography and architecture books as well as magazines and journals.

115 **L'EAU À LA BOUCHE** 35-37 Broadway Market, Hackney E8 4PH
020 7923 0600 www.labouche.co.uk

This cute café and deli is a favourite for families, hipsters and tourists. The French inspired menu includes delicious quiches, salads, baked goods and gourmet coffee.

BUEN AYRE 50 Broadway Market, Hackney E8 4QJ
020 7275 9900 www.buenayre.co.uk

Now legendary meat magnet in the heart of Broadway Market. Chunky chunky juicy juicy steak grilled by proud Irish-Argentinian dynasty.

117   **69B** 69b Broadway Market, Hackney E8 4PH
020 7249 9655 www.sixtynineb.com

Stylist, Merryn Leslie's edit of contemporary sustainable womenswear
brands as well as supporting new designer talent.

Labelled as the trendiest area in the world by Italian Vogue, Dalston lives up to its reputation of being fun, vibrant and on the forefront of everything new, particularly when it comes to fashion and nightlife. The weekends see the area hiving with activity from underground clubs to popular bars and hip restaurants. Visit in the day to explore the many vintage shops and cute cafés dotted along Kingsland Road.

INDEPENDENT DALSTON

HERE TODAY HERE TOMORROW 30a Balls Pond Road, Dalston N1 4AU
020 7241 0103 www.heretoday-heretomorrow.com

Passionate about sustainable ethical fashion, four local designers founded the hub/ showroom/boutique with inspired handmade collections of clothes and accessories.

123 MAMACHARI 18 Ashwin Street, Dalston E8 3DL
020 7254 0080 www.mamachari.co.uk

Selling recycled and refurbished traditional Japanese bikes, Mamachari offers a friendly workshop/repair service as well as vintage bike accessories and parts.

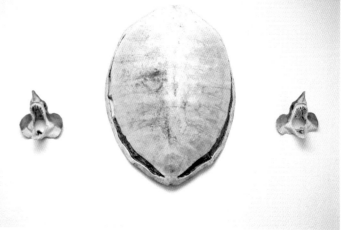

124 **HUNTER S** 194 Southgate Road, Dalston N1 3HT
020 7249 7191 www.thehunter-s.co.uk

Eye catching animals adorne the walls, exotic pictures hang in the toilets while a decent range of draft beers stock the bar, its a heady mix.

125 **PASSING CLOUDS** 1 Richmond Road, Dalston E8 4AA
020 7241 4889 www.passingclouds.org

Club and live music venue with principles supporting local and global projects.
Sonny Green pictured on the stage at Passing Clouds.

126 **THE PORTUGUESE CONSPIRACY** 55b King Henrys Walk, Dalston N1 4NH
020 7254 5813 www.theportugueseconspiracy.com

Conspiring to bring good food, wine and culture – it starting as a supper club in 2013 now an eatery, wine bar, deli and creative culture hub.

127 **WHITE RABBIT** 15–16 Bradbury Street, Dalston N16 8JN
020 7682 0163 www.whiterabbitdalston.com

With a contemporary and seasonal menu, this stylish minimalist restaurant serves a inspired selection of sharing plates, both big and small, all mouthwatering.

A circus-themed tiny concept store, at Fee Fee La Fou anything goes – including neon interiors, contemporary art and quirky handmade accessories and jewellery.

129 RIDLEY ROAD MARKET BAR 49 Ridley Road, Dalston E8 2NP

Serving delicious cocktails and Red Stripe beer, this tropical-themed bar with disco balls, a small dance floor and an ever-rotating selection of live music and DJs.

130 **STIGHLORGAN** 1 Stoke Newington Road, Dalston N16 8BH
020 3605 9401 www.stighlorgan.com

Irish accessories brand producing a wide array of quality bags, backpacks, drawstring bags, satchels and totes as well as a line of hats, scarves and belts.

131 L'ATELIER DALSTON 31 Stoke Newington Road, Dalston N16 8BJ
07540 570 288 @lAtelierDalston

Café by day, restaurant by night, L'Atelier has one of the chicest décors in East London. The European menu and stylish setting (for sale) make it a local favourite.

Still proudly underground, Lyal hosts a friendly melting pot of fashionistas, drag queens and late night party goers. Stay tuned for their varied events.

133 PELICANS AND PARROTS 40 Stoke Newington Road, Dalston N16 7XJ
020 3215 2083 www.pelicansandparrots.com

The neighbourhood lifestyle emporium, P & P is one of the most original über stylish boutiques in Dalston, with a beautifully curated mix of vintage fashion and interiors.

134 PELICANS AND PARROTS BLACK 81 Stoke Newington Road, Dalston N16 8AD
020 7249 9177 www.pelicansandparrots.com

Wondrous selection of vintage and new interiors, items on display at this unique boutique range from African tribal art, taxidermy, curios and industrial furniture.

135 **BELOW** 81 Stoke Newington Road, Dalston N16 8AD
020 7249 9177 www.pelicansandparrots.com

In a former Turkish social club, the basement 'Beach shack' is reminiscent of a Caribbean beach bar. Enter the hidden gem via a secret door in the Black boutique.

Lovingly referred to as 'Stokey' by locals, Stoke Newington is a multicultural area popular with families, bohemian types and the creative community. Church Street is perhaps the best known road of this charming neighbourhood, home to a selection of remarkable pubs and bars, independent interiors and vintage boutiques as well as small cafés and restaurants.

INDEPENDENT

Stoke Newington

140 OUI MADAME! 182 Stoke Newington Road N16 7NU
020 3674 2967 www.oui-madame.co.uk

This eclectic bistro offers a short but enticing menu of French food, wine and spirits.
The bohemian interiors and creative clientele make it perfect for people watching.

TI PI TIN 47 Stoke Newington High Street N16 8EL
www.tipitin.com

Promoting publications by contemporary artists, Ti Pi Tin sells a diverse selection of independent creative books, journals and zines with a focus on art and photography.

142 BLACK PIG WITH WHITE PEARLS 61 Stoke Newington High Street N16 8EL
020 7249 1772 www.blackpigwithwhitepearls.co.uk

A real taste of Spain in Stokey, at Black Pig with White Pearls you can enjoy
real Spanish tapas by candlelight accompanied by traditional Flamenco music.

143 LAZY SOCIAL 101 Stoke Newington High Street N16 0PH
020 7254 7684

Successfully fusing urban graffiti-covered walls with rustic wooden furniture,
this cozy café offers gourmet coffee, artisan cakes and mouthwatering breakfasts.

Specialising in ethical and eco-friendly yarns, this independent knitting shop
sells a range of accessories and books on hand knitting and crochet techniques.

145 OF CABBAGES & KINGS 127 Stoke Newington High Street N16 0PH
020 7998 3282 www.ofcabbagesandkings.co.uk

Focusing on British design, this contemporary art and crafts gallery sells a selection of prints by local artists and designers, as well as books, stationery and accessories.

146 KISSING IN TRAFFIC 155 Stoke Newington High Street N16 0NY
07904 541 269 www.kissingintraffic.com

Mixing colours and patterns with a distinct Dalston fashionista vibe, this unique boutique has a fabulous mix of handmade and vintage clothing with an urban edge.

ROUGE 158 Stoke Newington High Street N16 7JL
020 7275 0887 www.rouge-shop.co.uk

Inspired by artisan crafts and travel, Rouge houses a stunning array of interiors (vintage and new) and gifts from China, Mongolia, Japan, Thailand and Vietnam.

148 HABERDASHERY 170 Stoke Newington High Street N16 7JL
020 3643 7123 www.the-haberdashery.com

Award winning café housed in a former 30s butcher's has quickly become a local favourite. Serving made to order dishes with locally sourced produce.

Contemporary womenswear boutique houses stylish fashion labels including UK favourites Ally Capellino, Folk and YMC with a selection of Scandinavian brands.

A haven for stylish gentleman, the Hub menswear store stocks on-trend labels such British classics Oliver Spencer and Sunspel and Swedish heritage brand Our Legacy.

106 Stoke Newington Church Street N16 OLA
020 3556 8362 www.homageonline.co.uk

A truly unique interiors boutique, Homage carries a range of independent homeware brands including reclaimed furniture and contemporary minimalist ceramics.

Fusing gorgeous plants and beautiful hand tied bouquets with a small café,
Flowers N16 is a true sanctuary for flower enthusiasts and coffee connoisseur alike.

153 NOOK 153 Stoke Newington Church Street N16 0UH
020 7249 9436 www.nookshop.co.uk

This stylish design boutique offers a brilliant mix of lifestyle products, including Scandinavian interiors, contemporary stationery and a covetable edit of magazines.

A carefully curated selection of beautiful interiors, special gift items, stylish jewellery and contemporary stationery on display at this adorable lifestyle boutique.

HANSEN & LYDERSEN 3–5 Shelford Place N16 9HS
07927 363 397 www.hansen-lydersen.com

Salmon smoked in the city. Demanding standards, sustainable harvesting as well as the total care and attention to detail Ole shows to his product have made it a calling.

At the very heart of Hackney, Hackney Central is a multi-cultural melting pot with a diverse population and tightly knit local community. Home to a number of cultural venues including one of the oldest music halls in Britain, Hackney Empire – this eclectic area has recently seen an upsurge in the number of new independent boutiques, bars and eateries.

INDEPENDENT
HACKNEY

160 OSLO 1a Amhurst Road, Hackney E8 1LL
020 3553 4831 www.oslohackney.com

An example of new Hackney located inside the old Hackney Central station, Oslo is an event space, bar and restaurant inspired by Scandinavian minimalist aesthetics.

161 **CHASE & SORENSEN** 238d Dalston Lane, Hackney E8 1IQ
020 8533 5528 www.chaseandsorensen.com

Specialising in Scandinavian mid-century interiors, Chase & Sorensen sources its
furniture in Denmark with an ever-changing selection of contemporary classics.

PROPER OLD 173 Dalston Lane, Lower Clapton E8 1AL
07901 637 608   www.properold.com

Proper Old stocks an eclectic mix of antique interiors and art including unique furniture, lighting, ceramics and one-off collectable glass pieces.

HASH E8 170c Dalston Lane, Hackney E8 1NG
020 7254 0322 www.hashe8.com

This rustic diner and brunch bar serves a mouthwatering selection of British and American breakfast classics. Evening comfort menu of burgers, mac and cheese.

Quickly transforming into one of the most happening areas of Hackney, Lower Clapton offers an ever-evolving bar and food scene, unique shopping opportunities and a relaxed low-key vibe. Slightly off the beaten path, multi-cultural and diverse, this quaint area is home to Clapton Pond, the magnificent Georgian architecture of Clapton Square and the unusual Round Chapel dating back to the late 17th century.

INDEPENDENT
LOWER CLAPTON

A delightful mix of desirable comic books (both vintage and new)
as well collectable toys for big kids.

169 **UMIT & SON** 35 Lower Clapton Road, Lower Clapton E5 0NS
020 8985 1766 www.cine-real.com

Long established original on Lower Clapton. Challenge cine specialist and film fanatic Umit on his knowledge of kung fu movies... you'll lose.

BAD DENIM 82 Lower Clapton Road, Lower Clapton E5 0RN
07894 203 922   www.baddenim.co.uk

One-of-a-kind vintage styles to premium denim brands and independent labels,
on-trend jeans specialist Erin McQueen offers a stylish selection of everything denim.

171   ORIOLE & THISTLE 92 Lower Clapton Road, Lower Clapton E5 0QR
020 8986 8633 www.orioleandthistle.com

While also selling stunning hand-tied bouquets, this creative florist curates an ever-evolving gallery space showcasing the work of contemporary artists and designers.

KATE SHERIDAN 112 Lower Clapton Road, Lower Clapton E5 0QR
020 8985 7500 www.katesheridan.com

Independent label Kate Sheridan's signature pieces include minimalist-inspired handcrafted leather bags and accessories and fashion-forward waxed coats.

173 **WILD & WOOLLY** 116 Lower Clapton Road, Lower Clapton E5 0QR
020 8985 5231 www.wildandwoollyshop.co.uk

Offering a selection of knitting supplies, Wild and Woolly hosts regular workshops where you can practice (and perfect) your crochet, felting and knitting techniques.

174 **OTHER SIDE OF THE PILLOW** 161b Lower Clapton Road, Lower Clapton E5 8NB
07988 870 508 www.pillowheat.com

Browse an impressive selection of original old-school Vans as well as handpicked vintage eyewear and skate t-shirts at this unique Clapton shop.

175 **MAEVE'S KITCHEN** 181 Lower Clapton Road, Lower Clapton E5 8EQ
020 8533 1057 www.maeveskitchen.com

Rustic slow-cooked stews and a selection of delicious homemade one-pot dishes with delights such as Chicken with caramelised onions and cardonom rice.

DOM'S PLACE 199 Lower Clapton Road, Lower Clapton E5 8EG
020 8985 5454 www.doms-place.com

Classic Turkish cuisine with contemporary twist, the family-owned restaurant offers tasty kebab-inspired wraps, wine from Borough Wines, cocktails and craft beers.

177 CAVE OF PLUNDER 201 Lower Clapton Road, Lower Clapton E5 8EG
020 8986 9991 www.caveofplunder.com

Serving the best in comfort food, Cave of Plunder is a local diner offering milkshakes, pizzas and burgers. Try the ice cream sundae for the ultimate indulgence.

*Located in the middle of up-and-coming
Lower Clapton, Chatsworth Road is
a charming mix of Victorian architecture,
quaint eateries, local shops and independent
boutiques. The popular Sunday market
offers a delightful mix of artisan food, retro
homeware and vintage clothing – attracting
a diverse crowd of trendy locals, families
and the odd tourist.*

INDEPENDENT
CHATSWORTH
ROAD

182 HATCH 8 Mackintosh Lane, Homerton E9 6AB
020 8533 5007 www.hatch-homerton.co.uk

This creative, multi-purpose space offers a café/bar, desk hire and regular pop-up events. The grand windows and antique furniture (for sale) lend a bohemian touch.

183 **THE PLOUGH** 23–25 Homerton High Street, Homerton E9 6JP
020 8986 8433 www.hackneyplough.co.uk

A contemporary and charming pub serving locally sourced and international craft beers, wine and cocktails (mainly based around American Whiskies and Tequilas).

184 BOTANY 5 Chatsworth Road, Homerton E5 0LH
020 8986 8433 www.hackneyplough.co.uk

A green haven, this adorable lifestyle boutique is home to an impressive variety of succulents, cacti and houseplants as well as gorgeous stationery and tableware.

185 **SHANE'S ON CHATSWORTH** 62 Chatsworth Road, Homerton E5 OLS
020 8985 3755 www.shanesonchatsworth.com

Contemporary British cuisine with a focus on local ingredients, Shane's has an ever-changing seasonal menu with a good selection of game, seafood and cheese.

186 TRIANGLE 92a Chatsworth Road, Homerton E5 0LS
07929 410 263 www.trianglestore.co.uk

An enchanting assortment of beautiful interiors items (both vintage and new), gifts and accessories. This diminutive boutique houses a grand selection for the home.

187 COOPER & WOLF 145 Chatsworth Road, Homerton E5 OLS
07830 495 048 www.cooperandwolf.co.uk

Scandinavian treats (cinnamon buns and traditional baked goods) are served at this cute café. The retro-inspired interior makes a cozy spot for coffee, lunch or brunch.

Slightly forgotten and perhaps not as loved as many other East London areas, Bethnal Green offers an interesting multi-cultural mix of local grocery stores, eateries and artist's studios. The Bethnal Green Museum of Childhood displays a magnificent selection of old toys and other childhood related objects, an intriguing part of history for young as well as old.

INDEPENDENT

Roman Road

PRICK YOUR FINGER 260 Globe Road E2 0JD
020 8981 2560 www.prickyourfinger.com

Inspired by Punk Rock and the Arts & Craft movement, Prick Your Finger is a yarn shop and textile collective offering both knitting supplies and monthly workshops.

192 ANCHOR + HOPE 363 Roman Road E3 5QR
07825 041 218 www.anchorandhopelondon.co.uk

Pre-loved recycled fashion, at Anchor + Hope you'll find both high street labels and designer names as well as London's largest selection of secondhand maternity wear.

193 **THE VICTORIA** 110 Globe Road E3 5TH
020 8712 5125 www.thevicmileend.co.uk

Re-vamped classic East End pub specialising in alternative music, serving a
mouthwatering selection of burgers, Saturday brunch and traditional Sunday roast.

Specialising in contemporary gifts and small design objects, Snap is an independent boutique stocking a stylish selection of cards, stationery, books and prints.

MUXIMA 618 Roman Road E3 2RW
020 8980 0850 www.muxima.co.uk

Serving artisan coffee and food, this art and culture café/bar promotes local and
international artists through a dynamic program of exhibitions and creative events.

Located just seconds from one of London's biggest and most beautiful parks, Victoria Park Village is a charming mix of local gastro pubs, independent boutiques and artisan food shops and gourmet delis. This leafy part of East London provides a welcome break from the hustle and bustle of city living with Lauriston Road and Victoria Park Road housing a plethora of appealing shopping opportunities.

INDEPENDENT

VICTORIA
VILLAGE

199 THE TOYBOX 223 Victoria Park Road E9 7HD
020 8533 2879 www.thetoyboxshop.co.uk

Been invited to a kids' party? This is the perfect spot to pick up a present including fun and colourful toys, Lego, board games and cute cards for the smallest ones.

200 BRANCH IN THE PARK 227 Victoria Park Road E9 7HD
020 8533 7977 www.branchonthepark.co.uk

Founded by local goldsmith Julia Cook in 2010, this tranquil jewellery store offers
a mix of bespoke signature pieces featuring precious and semi-precious stones.

With wooden floors and rustic reclaimed furniture, this charming café is the perfect spot to pick up fresh bread, pastries, delicious cakes and local Monmouth coffee.

Celebrating authentic Mexican cuisine, this cozy restaurant serves a mouthwatering selection of nachos, burritos and tacos as well as classic tequila-based cocktails.

203 BOTTLE APOSTLE 95 Lauriston Road E9 7HJ
020 8985 1549 www.bottleapostle.com

Award-winning artisan wine shop, Bottle Apostle stocks a remarkable range of wine, craft beers and ciders as well as hosting popular winetasting events and workshops.

204 THE EMPRESS 130 Lauriston Road E9 7LH
020 8533 5123 www.empresse9.co.uk

Focusing on contemporary British cuisine, The Empress serves an impressive
seasonally changing menu with mainly locally sourced ingredients.

205 HAUS 39 Morpeth Road London E9 7LD
020 7536 9291 www.hauslondon.com

Small yet bursting with style, Haus stocks an inspiring selection of international (mainly Scandinavian and Northern European) and British contemporary interiors.

This urban area is an intriguing mix of warehouses, industrial estates and factory buildings. Still slightly eerie and desolate, Hackney Wick has benefitted from the 2012 Olympics investment and is home to a small selection of hip eateries, galleries and artist studios. The close proximity to the River Lea, Victoria Park and Hackney Marshes makes it a popular weekend destination for Londoners in the know.

INDEPENDENT

HACKNEY
WICK

210 IMPERIAL & STANDARD 10 Felstead Street, Hackney Wick E9 5LT
07754 553 778 www.imperialandstandard.com

Specialising in Victorian antiques, industrial furniture and 20th century collectables and fixings, Imperial & Standard offers a splendid selection of vintage interiors.

211 **VINYL PIMP** 14 Felstead Street, Hackney Wick E9 5LT
020 8986 5943 www.vinylpimp.co.uk

Ranked as one of the best record stores in town by DJs and music professionals,
Vinyl Pimp stocks an impressive collection of rare disco, funk, breakbeat and house.

212 **THE YARD THEATRE** Unit 2a, Queen's Yard, Hackney Wick E9 5EN
07548 156 266 www.theyardtheatre.co.uk

In a converted warehouse, this 110-seat theatre venue (with a kitchen and bar) was
built using reclaimed materials with the concrete floor lending a distinct urban edge.

213 **CRATE BREWERY** The White Building, Queen's Yard, Hackney Wick E9 5LT
07834 275 687 www.cratebrewery.com

One of the coolest industrial venues in Hackney, this popular canal side craft brewery offers a mouthwatering menu of pizzas and lovingly brewed beer.

Dedicated to handbuilt custom motorbikes, good food, coffee and beer – the showroom cum-café also sells a small selection of bike gear and accessories.

COUNTER CAFÉ 7 Roach Road, Hackney Wick E9 5LT
07834 275 920 www.counterproductive.co.uk

Located just by the Lea navigation with impressive views across to the Olympic Stadium, this quirky warehouse café serves terrific breakfast, brunch and coffee.

Located a bit further north (in zone 3) is Walthamstow, a slightly more suburban East End area, yet with a growing hip factor. Walthamstow Village boasts a multitude of independent shops, pubs and restaurants, with Walthamstow Market being the longest street market in Europe. Home to a variety of galleries and creative ventures, this area has seen house prices double in the past couple of years and is dubbed as one of London's most desirable up-and-coming residential areas.

WALTHAMSTOW

220 BLACKDUKE & CASHMAN 83 Grove Road, Walthamstow E17 9BU
07947 895 015 www.blackdukeandcashman.com

Wonderful collection of British and Scandinavian furniture and design objects
from the 1950s–70s along individual unique art pieces from craft guerrilla.

221 **GODS OWN JUNKYARD** Ravenswood Industrial Estate, Shernhall St. E9 5LT
020 8521 8066 www.godsownjunkyard.co.uk

Situated on an industrial estate, this gallery-bar-café specialist store of remarkable antique and new neon signs, lights and movie props is like no where else.

222 **THE VIKING STORE** 119 Wood Street, Walthamstow E17 3LL
08432 896 520 www.thevikingstore.co.uk

One stop shop for the viking, celt, saxon or ork in you. Get tooled and costumed
to museum standards or LARP, 'live action role play' if you didn't already know.

223 BYGGA BO 8 Chingford Road, Walthamstow E17 4PJ
020 8527 3652 www.byggabo.com

In a former 70s hair salon, this Swedish café serves authentic Nordic cuisine as well as stocking a handpicked mix of Scandinavian design objects and kids clothes.

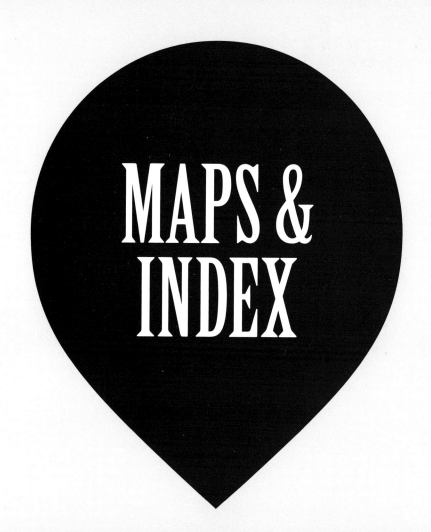

Shoreditch

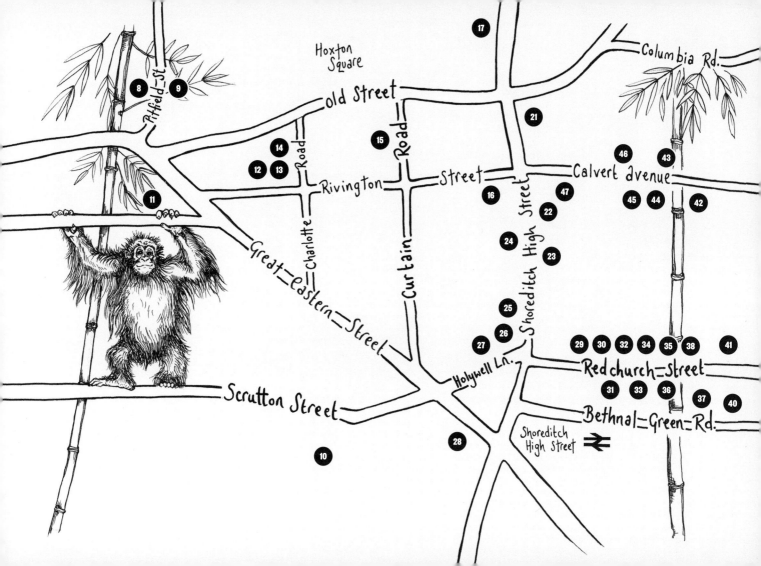

Dalston

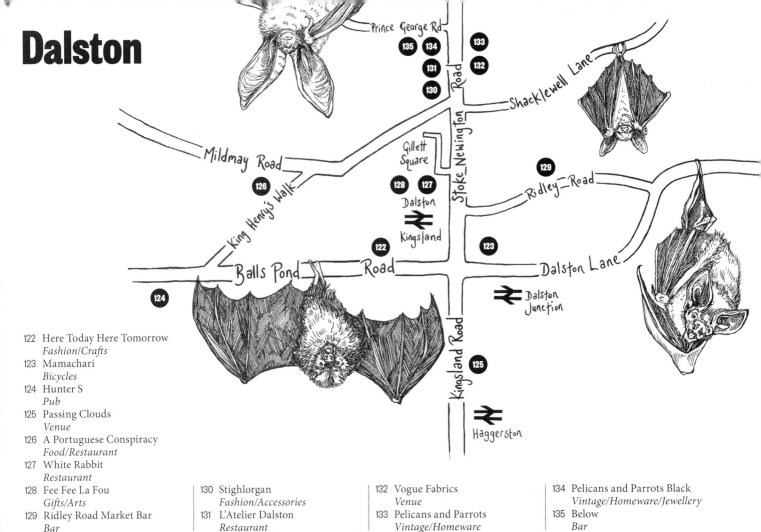

Prince George Rd
135 **134** **133**
131 **132**
130

Stoke Newington Road

Shacklewell Lane

Mildmay Road

King Henry's Walk

Gillett Square

126

128 **127**
Dalston

129
Ridley Road

⇄ Kingsland

122

123

Balls Pond Road

Dalston Lane

124

⇄ Dalston Junction

Kingsland Road

125

⇄ Haggerston

122 Here Today Here Tomorrow
Fashion/Crafts
123 Mamachari
Bicycles
124 Hunter S
Pub
125 Passing Clouds
Venue
126 A Portuguese Conspiracy
Food/Restaurant
127 White Rabbit
Restaurant
128 Fee Fee La Fou
Gifts/Arts
129 Ridley Road Market Bar
Bar

130 Stighlorgan
Fashion/Accessories
131 L'Atelier Dalston
Restaurant

132 Vogue Fabrics
Venue
133 Pelicans and Parrots
Vintage/Homeware

134 Pelicans and Parrots Black
Vintage/Homeware/Jewellery
135 Below
Bar

Brick Lane Spitalfields

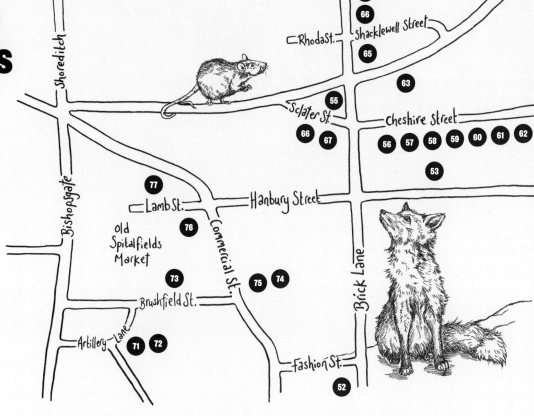

Broadway Market
Columbia Road

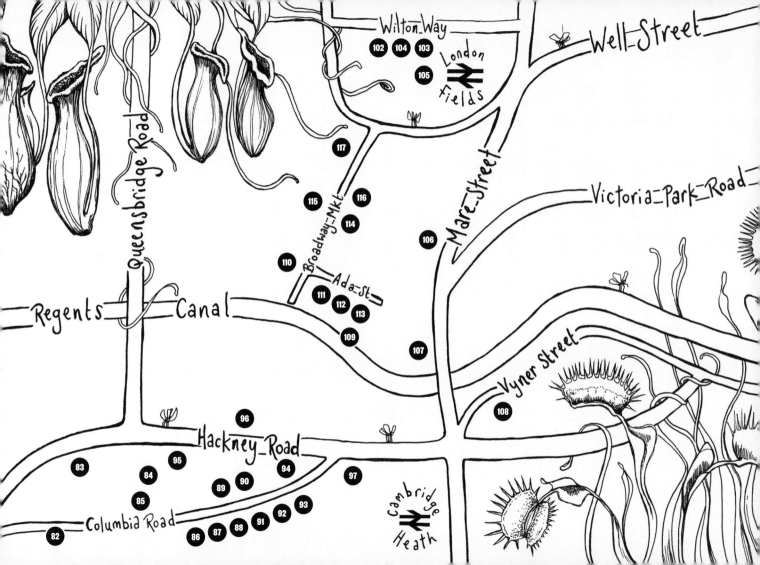

Victoria Village
Roman Road
Hackney Wick

Street

Mare

Regents — Canal

Bethnal Green

Globe Rd.

Hackney
Lower Clapton
Chatsworth Road

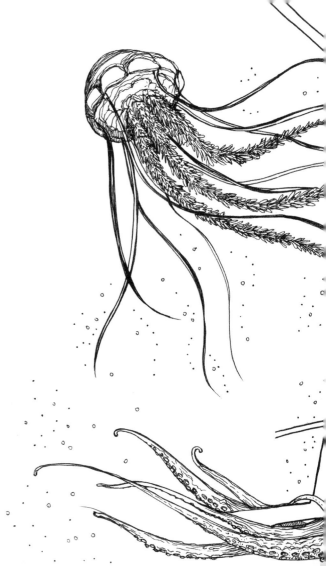

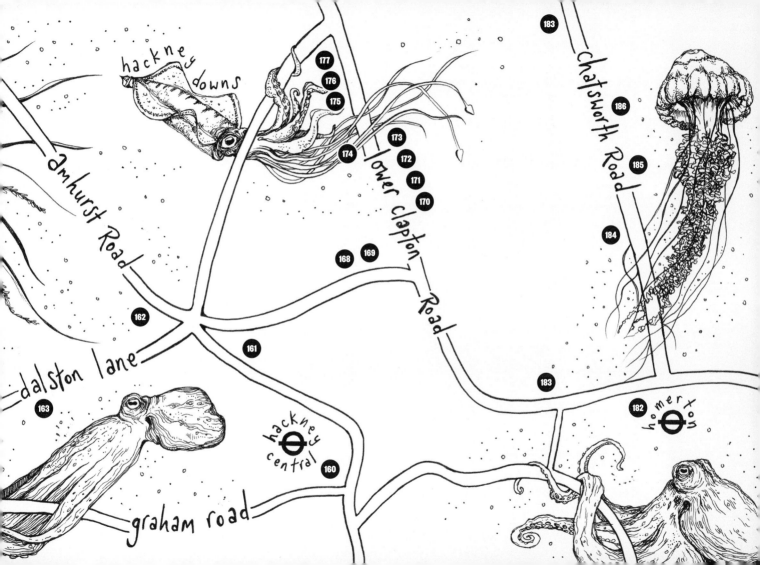

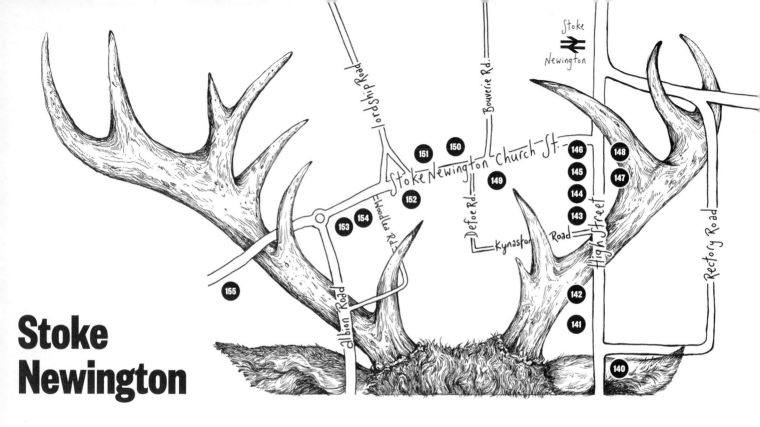

Stoke Newington

Walthamstow

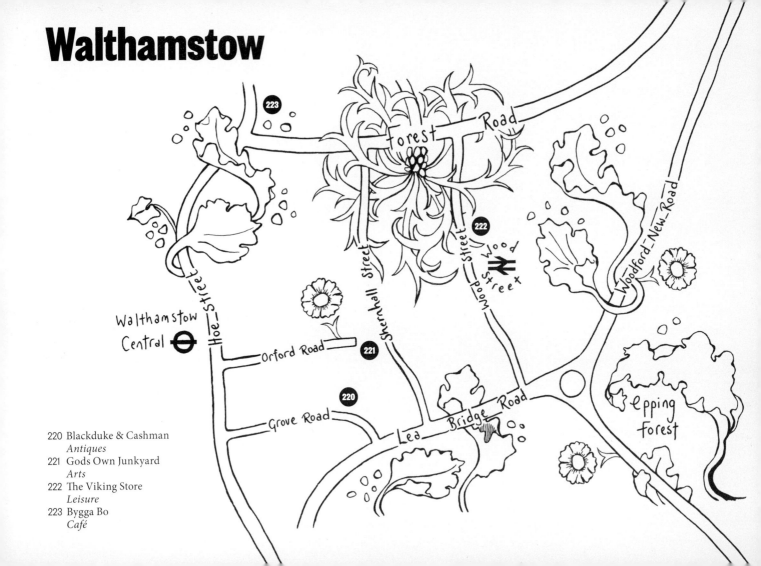

Index

Many thanks to all the independent owners and managers for their participation in this book

Design by Tim Fellowes
www.timfellowes.com

Reviews by Anna Jacobsen
www.wearehere-now.com

Illustrations by Jennie Webber
www.jenniewebber.com

Photography by Moritz Steiger and Effie Fotaki
guide@independentlondon.com
www.independentlondon.com

Copyright ©2014 Moritz Steiger and Effie Fotaki. All rights reserved

Published by MONSTERMEDIA